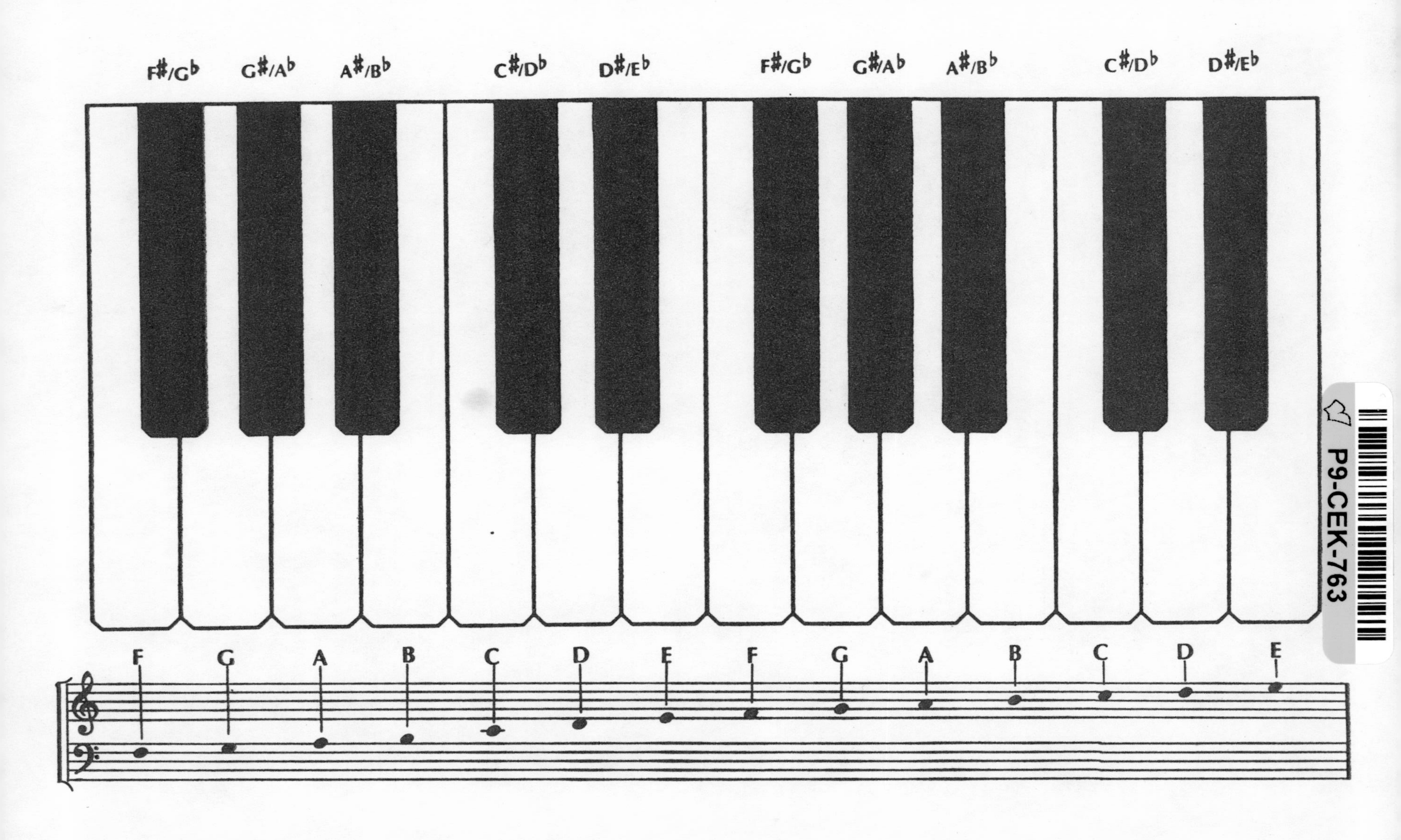
F#/Gb
G#/Ab
A#/Bb
C#/Db
D#/Eb
F#/Gb
G#/Ab
A#/Bb
C#/Db
D#/Eb
F G A B C D E F G A B C D E

Silver Burdett music

Centennial Edition

Elizabeth Crook

Bennett Reimer

David S. Walker

SILVER BURDETT COMPANY MORRISTOWN, NEW JERSEY

ATLANTA, GA · CINCINNATI, OH · DALLAS, TX · NORTHFIELD, IL · SAN CARLOS, CA · AGINCOURT, ONTARIO

ISBN 0-382-05922-0

Contents

MUSIC MEANS . . .

Sing

Move

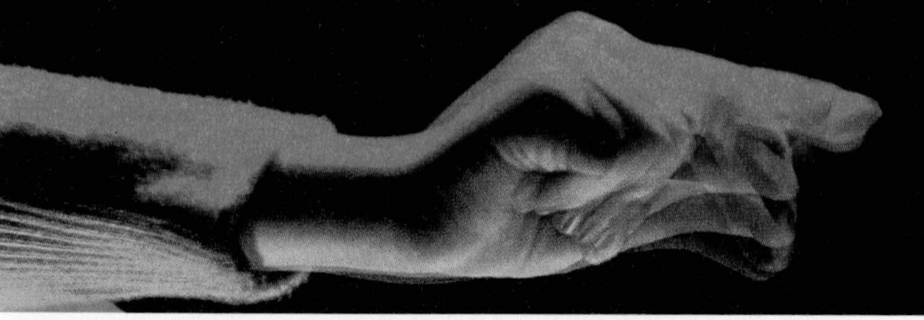

MUSIC MEANS . . .

Listen

Play

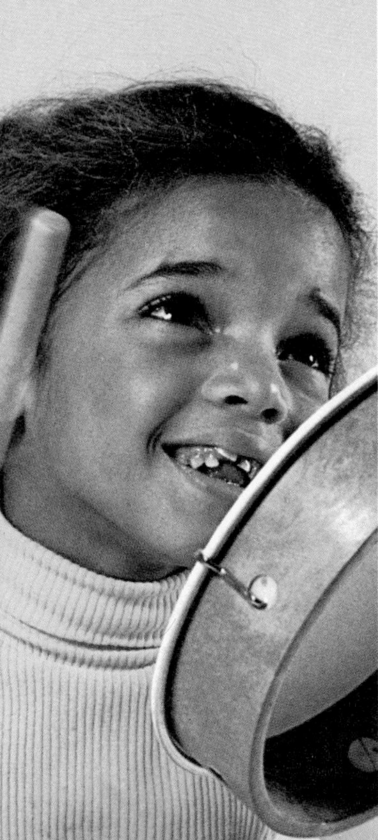

FAST AND SLOW

People, animals, and things move.

Fast

Slow

LOUD AND SOFT

Which sounds are **loud**?
Which sounds are **soft**?

LONG AND SHORT

Make a **long** motion.

Make a **short** motion.

bullets
42

A SOUND PIECE

FOOTPATH

Joyce Bogusky-Reimer

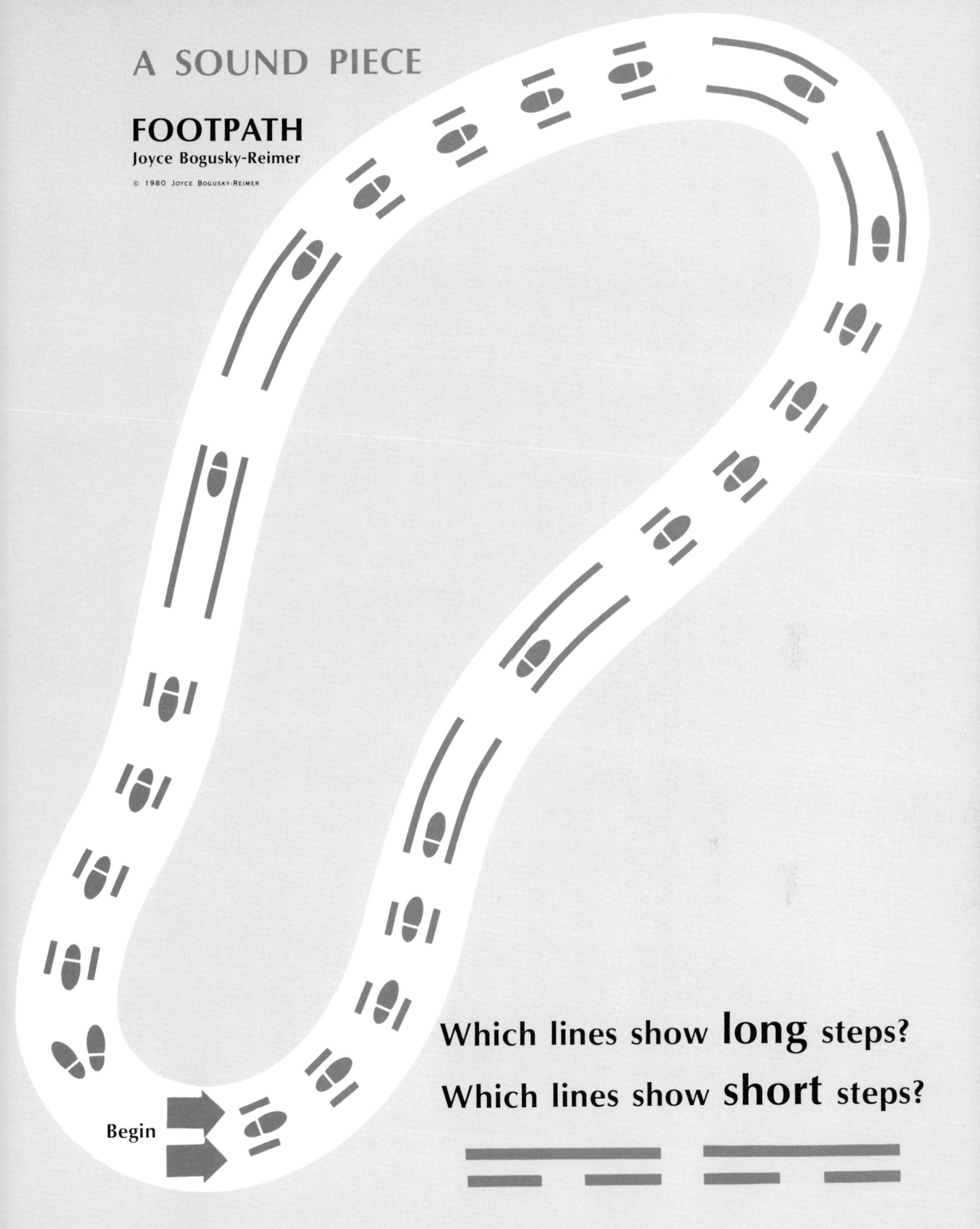
Begin

Which lines show long steps?

Which lines show short steps?

HIGH AND LOW

high

Reach **high.**

Reach **low.**

Play **high** sounds.

Play **low** sounds.

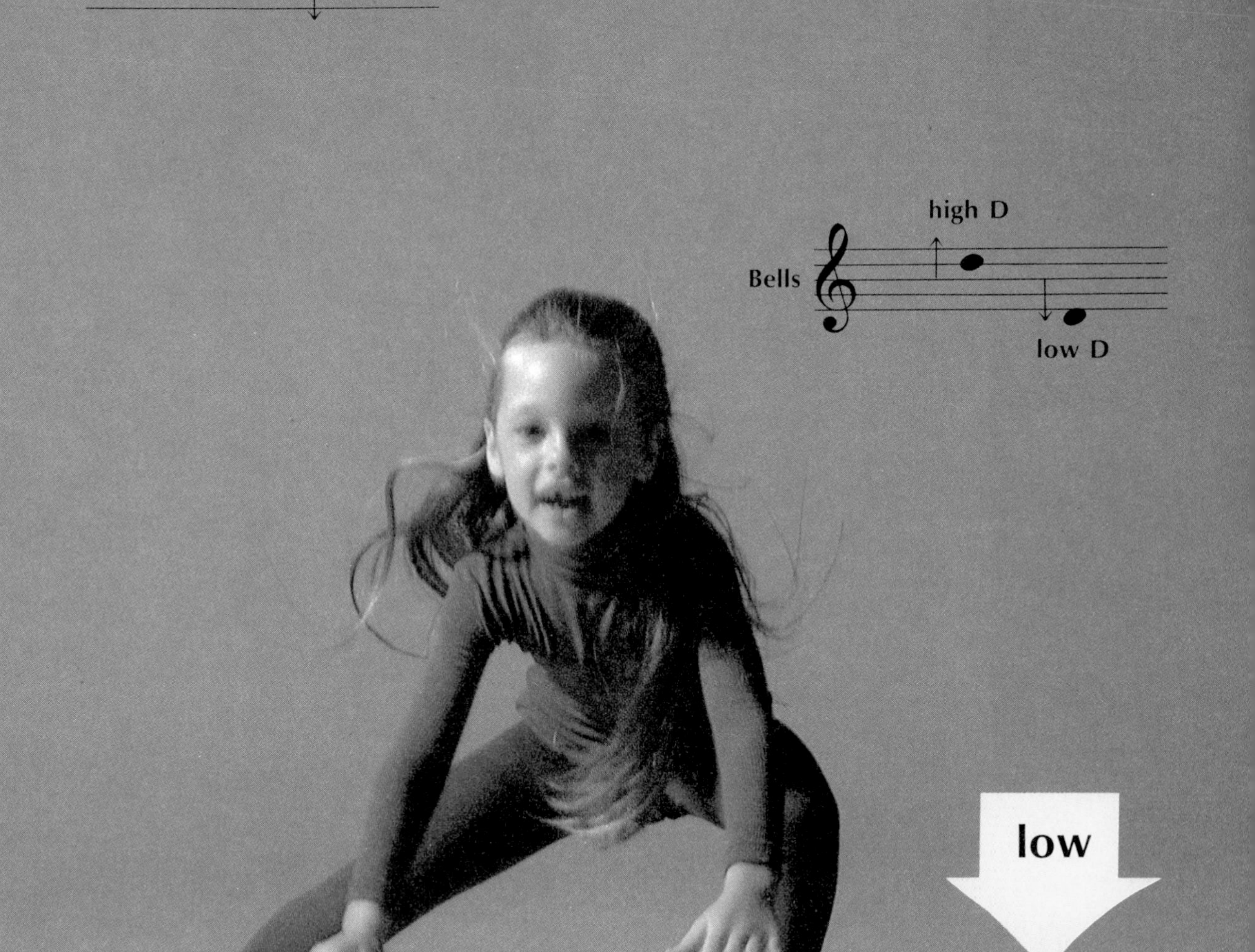
high D
Bells
low D
low

HIGH AND LOW ON INSTRUMENTS

Who is playing high sounds?

Who is playing low sounds?

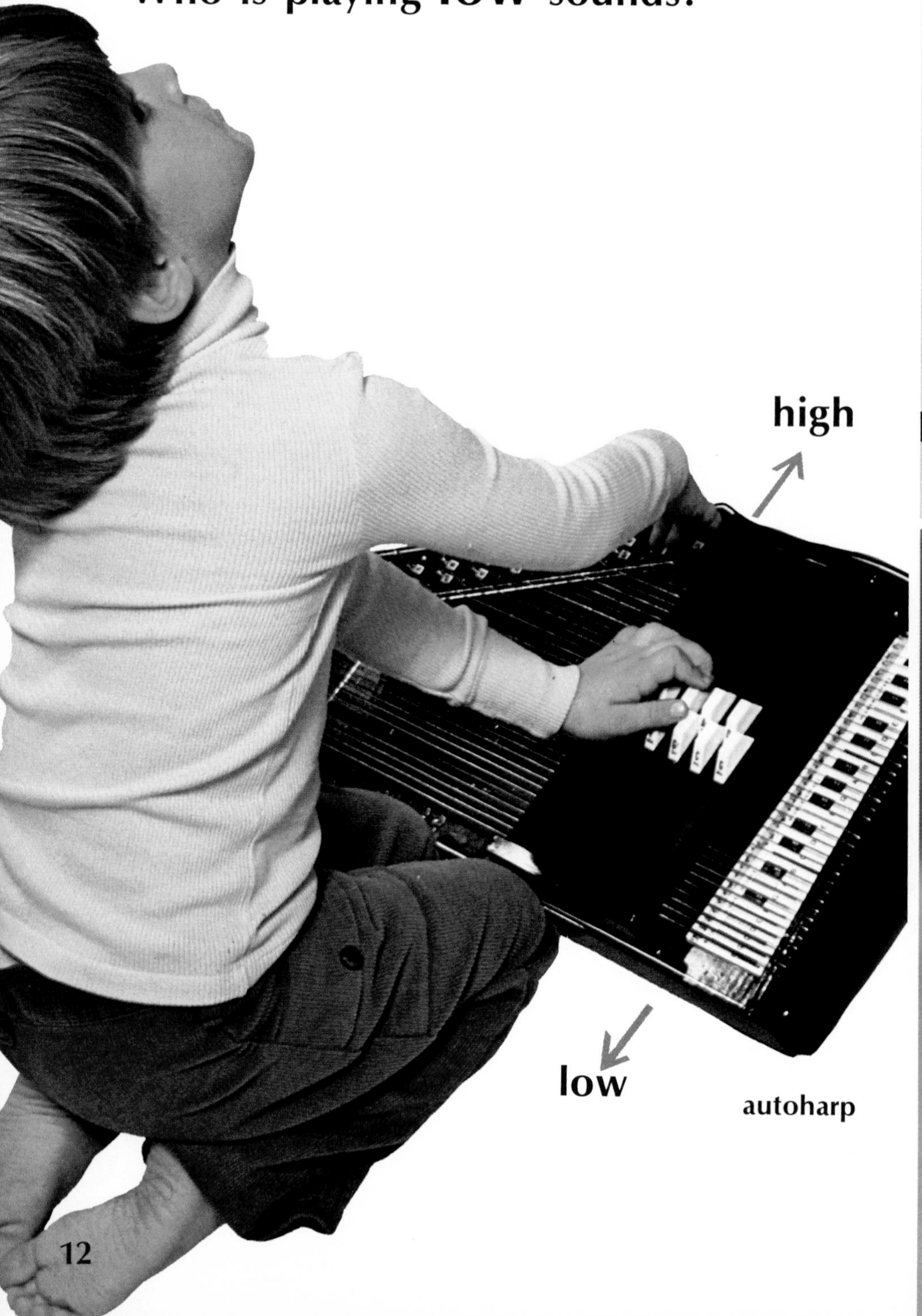
high
low

autoharp

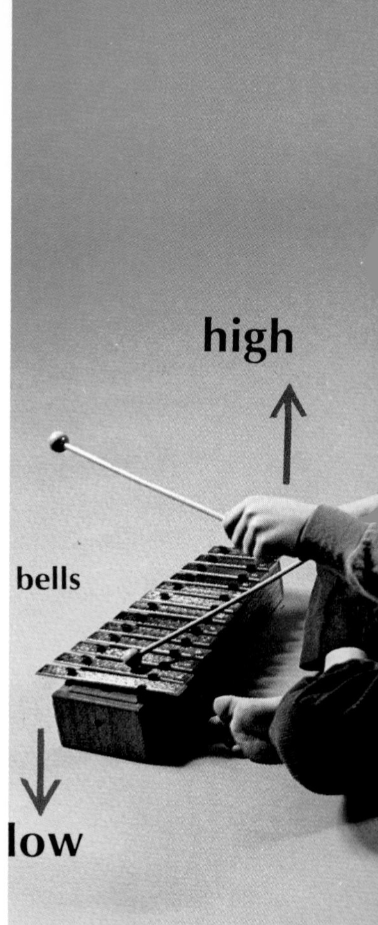
high
low

bells

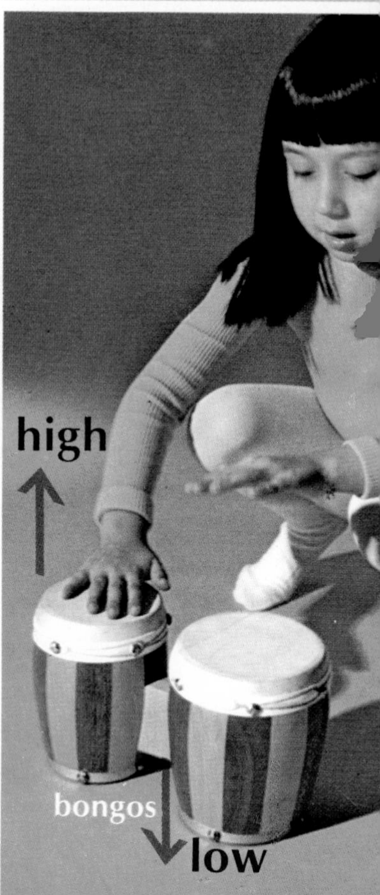
high
low

bongos

Play high and low sounds.
high C
Bells
low C
piano

KEEPING THE BEAT

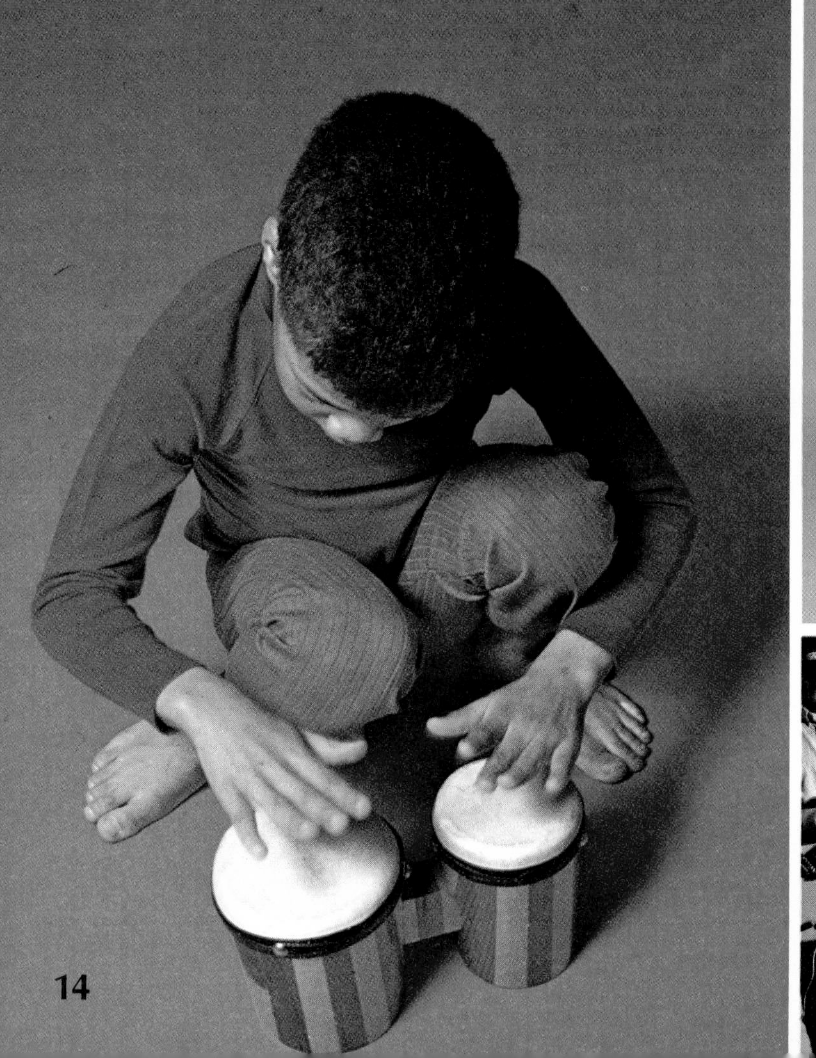

What is happening in each picture?

Match the pictures with the sounds you hear.

STEADY BEAT

These games use a steady beat.

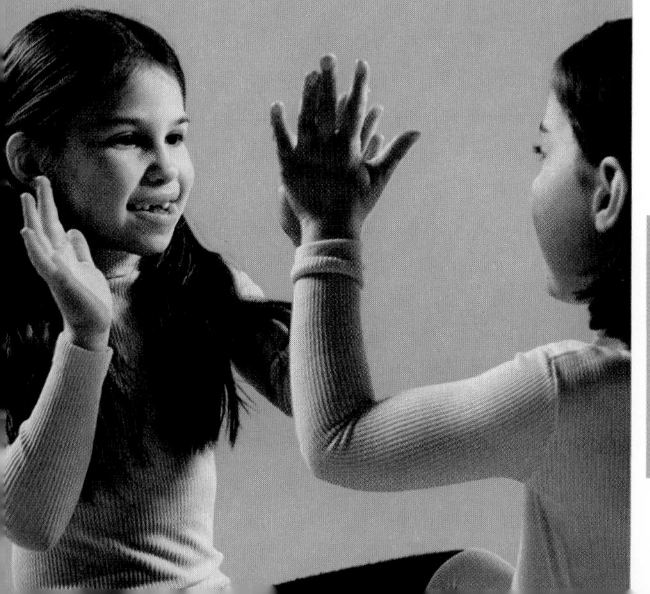

Some music has a steady beat.

NO BEAT

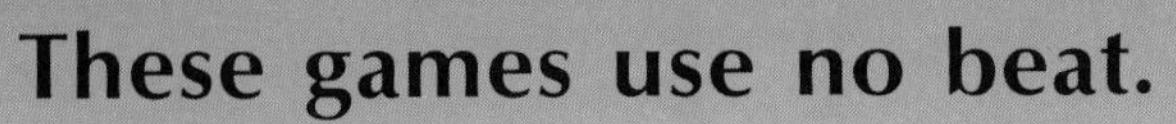

These games use no beat.

Some music has no beat.

JOHN MARIN, "CIRCUS ELEPHANTS," COLLECTION OF THE ART INSTITUTE OF CHICAGO.

Pictures can show the same thing in different ways.

AB FORM

Play loud sounds on a drum.

Play soft sounds on other instruments.

How are the pictures different?

How are the sounds different?

These shapes show that you played two different things.

These letters show that you played two different things.

You played music in AB form.

ABA FORM

Get on board!

Which pictures are the same?

Which picture is different?

How do the shapes match the pictures?

How do the letters match the pictures?

A B A

"Get on Board" is in ABA form.

STYLE

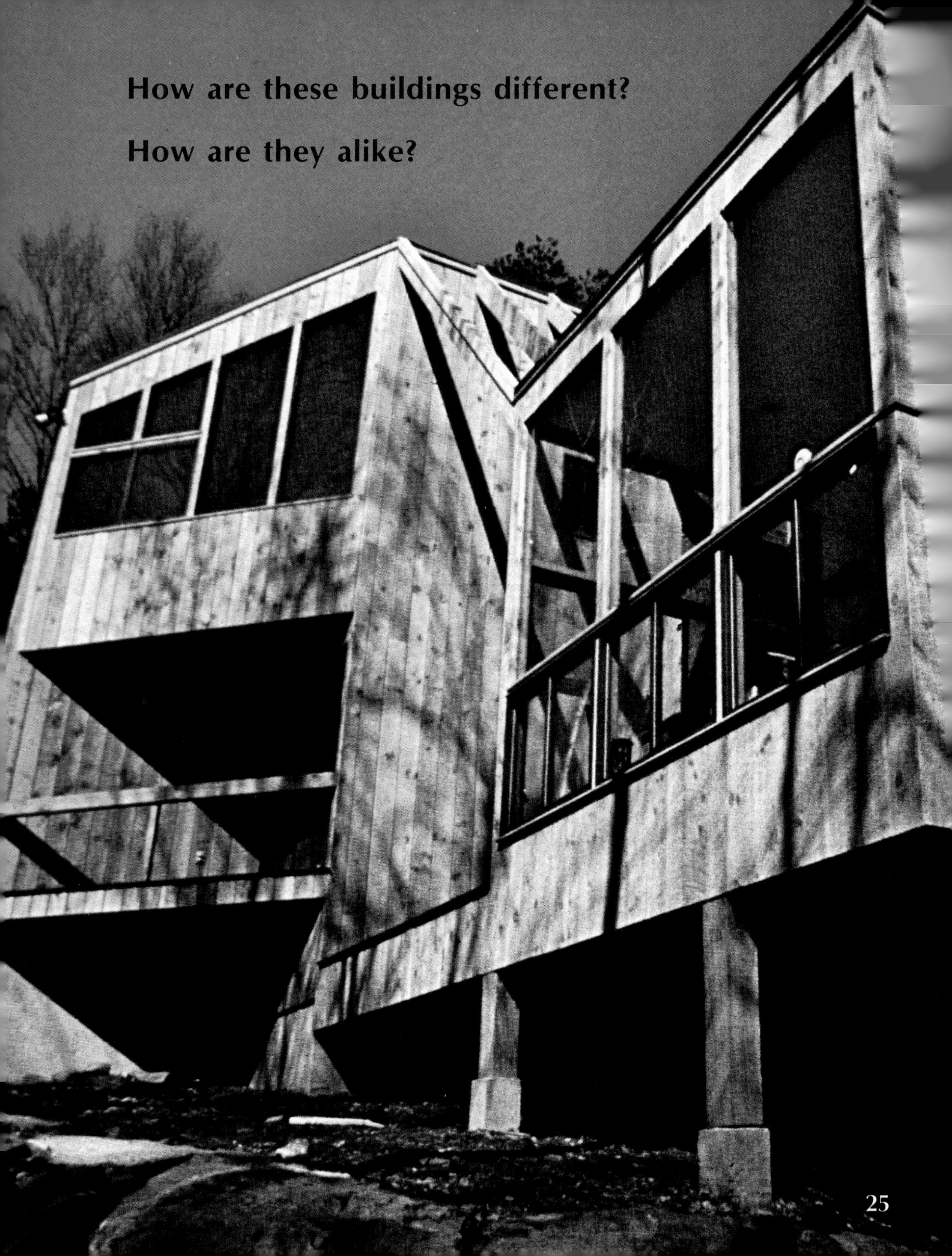

How are these buildings different?

How are they alike?

THE ARTS

Which movement is high?

Which movement is low?

THE ARTS

Find the high things in this painting.

Find the low things.

冨嶽三十六景
神奈川沖浪裏

"The Great Wave." The Metropolitan Museum of Art. Bequest of Mrs. H. O. Havemeyer, 1929. The H. O. Havemeyer Collection.

HOW BEATS MOVE

1. | | | | | |

2. | | | | | | | | | | | |

3. | | | | | | | | | | |

Which lines show the steady beat? The beat getting faster? The beat getting slower?

WORKING WITH SOUNDS

Match the pictures with the sounds you hear.

Play steady beats on bells.

high C

bells

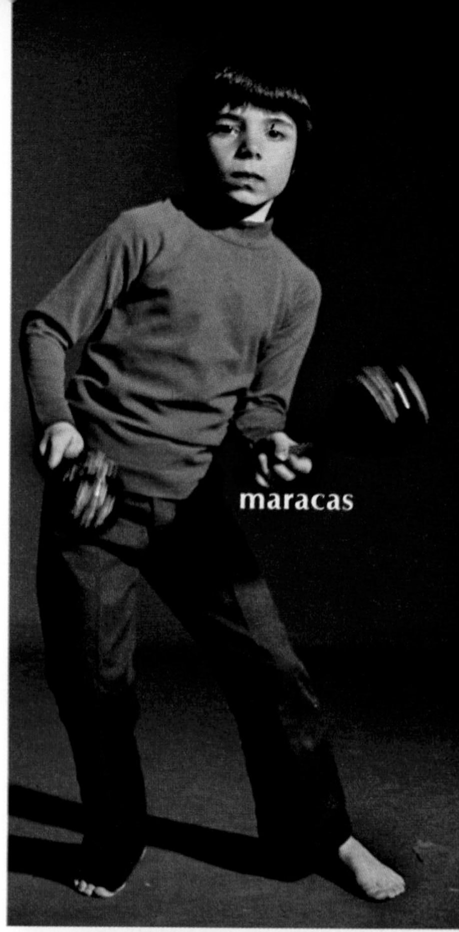
maracas

man's voice

wood block

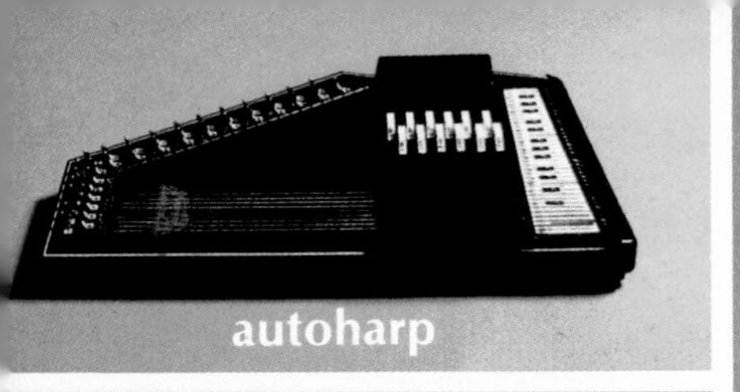
autoharp

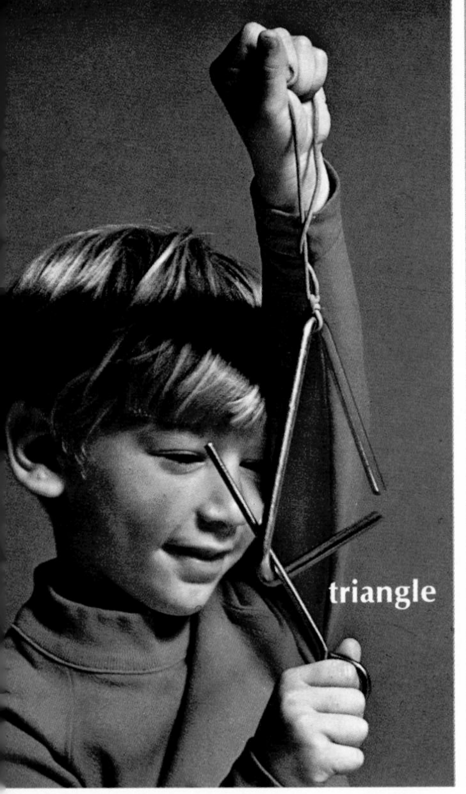
triangle

finger cymbals

drum

Play steady beats on a drum.

MORE ABOUT SOUNDS

flute

guitar

drums

trumpet

violin

Match the pictures with the sounds you hear.

THE ARTS

Name the colors you see in this painting.

ACCENTS

Which child is pointed out in each row?

This mark is an accent. >

Show the accents with your voice.

1. I HEAR the drummer strike the sky.

2. I hear the DRUMMER strike the sky.

3. I hear the drummer STRIKE the sky.

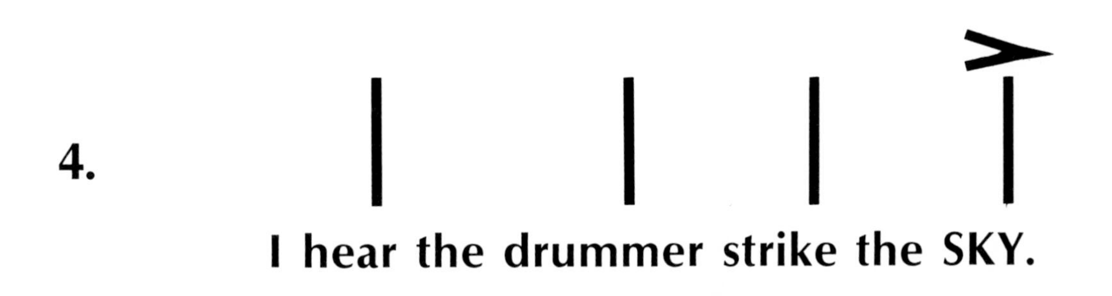

4. I hear the drummer strike the SKY.

BEATS IN SETS OF TWO

How does the picture show sets of two?

How do the lines show sets of two?

Notes can also show sets of two.

BEATS IN SETS OF THREE

How does the picture show sets of three?

How do the lines show sets of three?

Notes can also show sets of three.

HOW TONES MOVE

upward
Ev - 'ry - bod - y wants to sing!
O - hi - o.

downward

upward
and
downward
Hal - le - lu - jah!

DOWNWARD

Play downward sounds on the bells.

The Cricket's Song

Folk Song from the Ukraine   English Words by Leo R. Israel

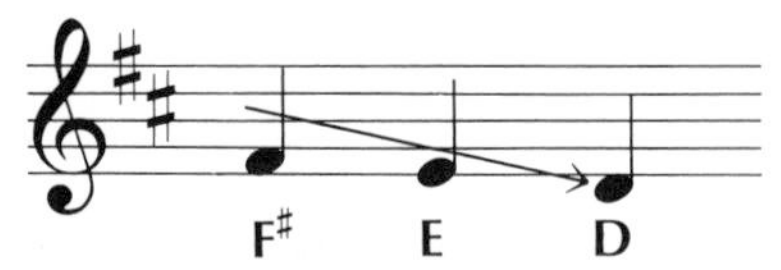
F♯
E
D

Ev'rything is silent but the crick-et's song,

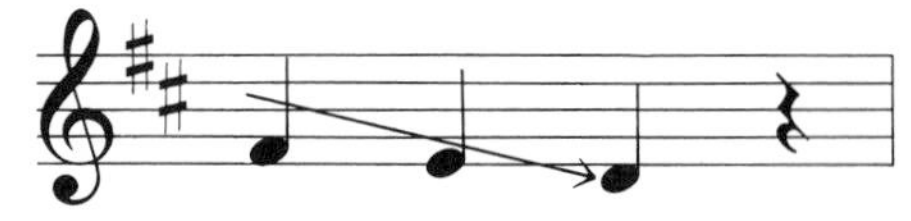

But the cricket's, but the cricket's, but the crick-et's song.

While the rest are busy he sings all day long,

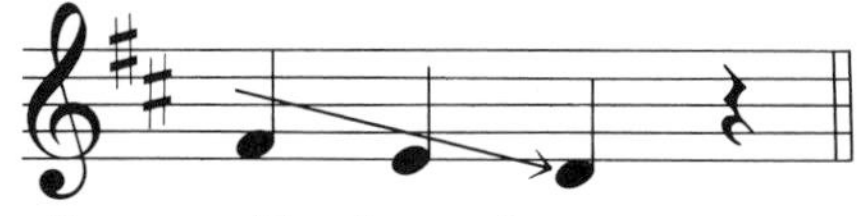

Singing all day, singing all day, singing all day long.

UPWARD AND DOWNWARD

Play sounds that move upward and downward.

That Is What He Say

American Folk Song

"Tell Me What the Jaybird Say," melody and words from Record No. 4057, AFS, Library of Congress.

1. Jay bird say, "Jay, jay, jay,"
2. Mockingbird say, "Whee, dee, dee,"
3. Chee dee say, "Chee, dee, dee,"
4. Old crow say, "Crah, crah, crah,"
5. Old hawk say, "Chick, chick, chick,"
6. Partridge say, "Bob, bob, white,"
7. Old owl say, "Whoo, whoo, whoo,"

C D E D C

That is what he say.

SONG ENDINGS

Here are endings of songs you know.

F#
D#
C#
A#
G#
F#
D#
C#
C
B
A
G
F
E
D
C

Find an ending that moves upward.

Find an ending that moves downward.

Find one that moves upward and downward.

1. 
Ev - 'ry - bod - y wants to sing!

2. 
Smashed to piec - es on the ground.

3. 
buy mo-las-ses can - dy.

4. 
Maw-ga Nan-ny show me how the ball goes roun'.

5. 
Hal - le - lu - jah!

THE ARTS

What lines do you see in this painting?

The Solomon R. Guggenheim Museum, New York. Paul Klee, "In the Current Six Thresholds," 1929

What lines do you see in this building?

RHYTHM PATTERNS

Clap these patterns of long and short sounds.

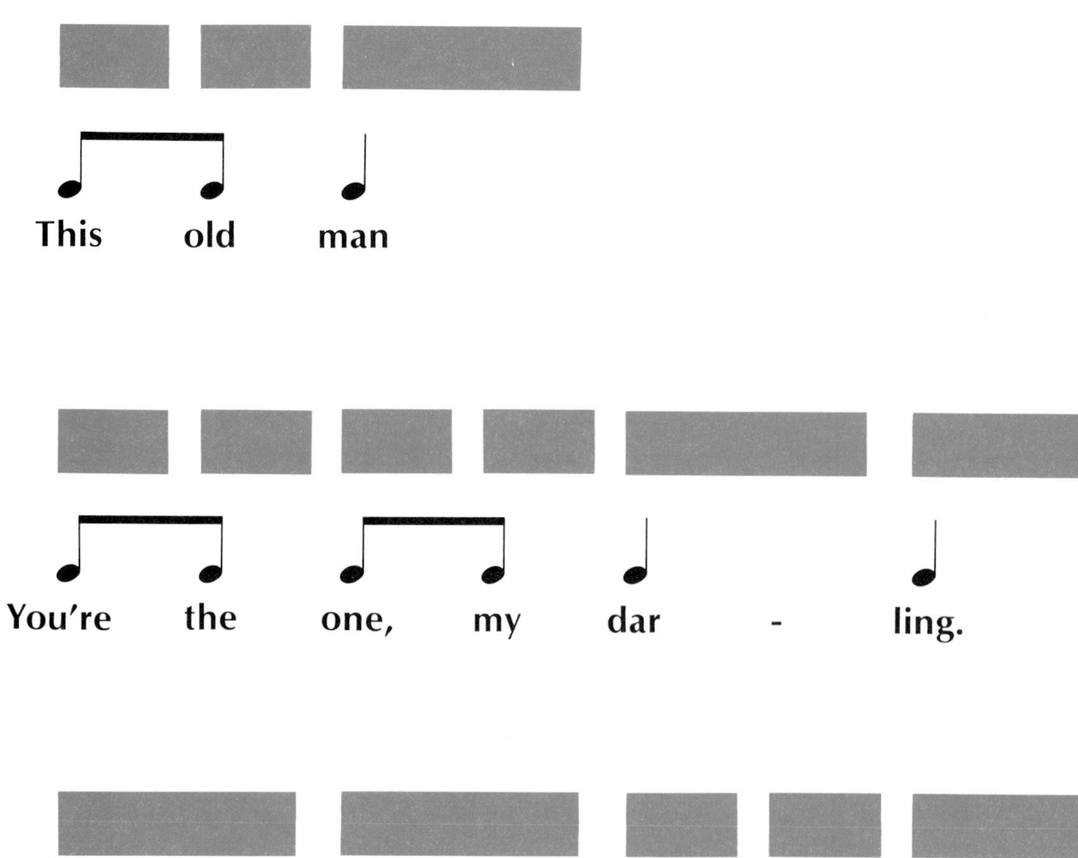
This old man
You're the one, my dar - ling.

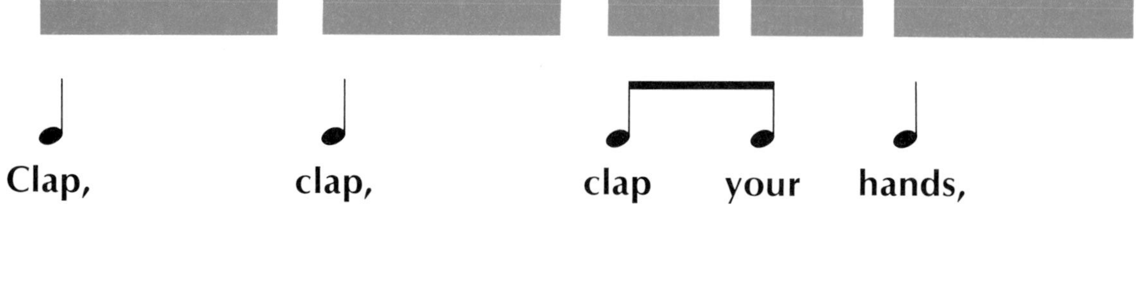
Clap, clap, clap your hands,

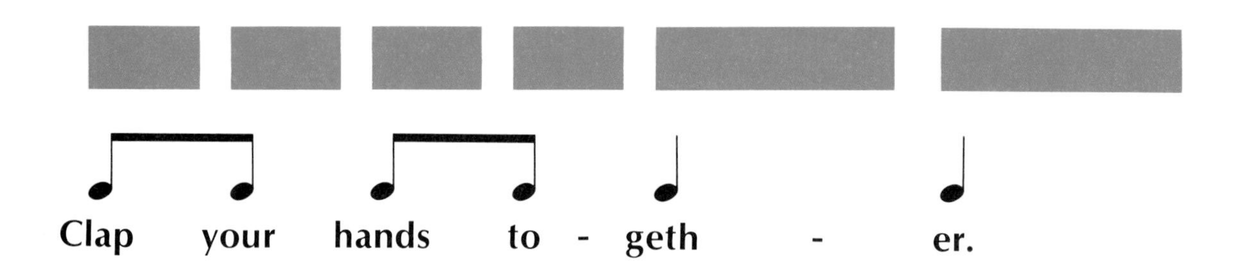
Clap your hands to - geth - er.

READING RHYTHM PATTERNS

Which patterns are alike?
Which patterns are different?

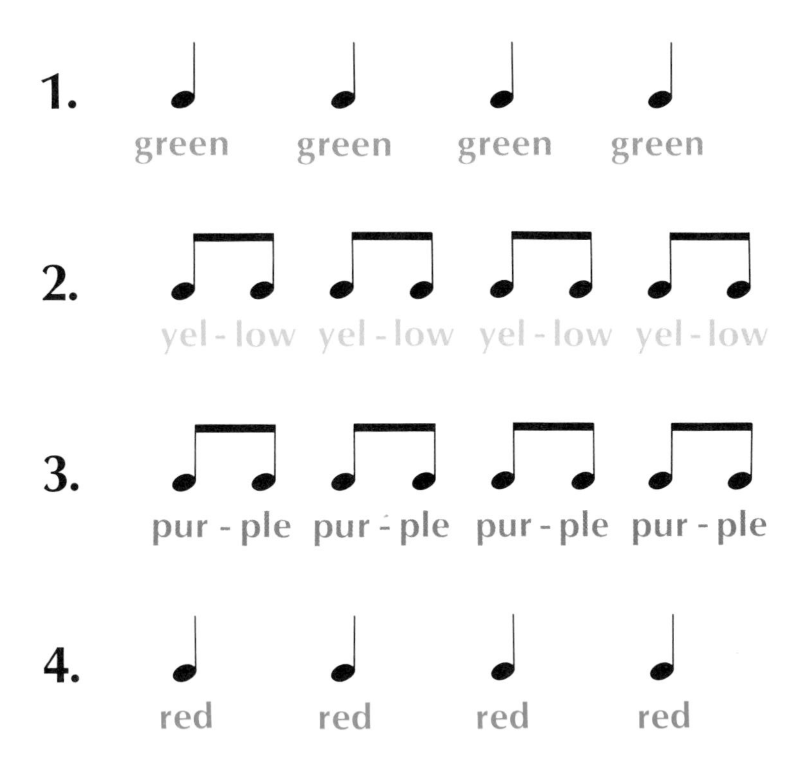
1.
green green green green
2.
yel - low yel - low yel - low yel - low
3.
pur - ple pur - ple pur - ple pur - ple
4.
red red red red

Can you read words?
Can you read rhythm patterns?

1. cir - cus cir - cus

2. el - e-phants el - e-phants

3. dogs do-ing danc - es

4. jug-gler on a tight - rope

RHYTHM PATTERNS IN A SONG

Read rhythm patterns in this song.

Great Big Stars

Black Spiritual

Great big stars 'way up yonder,

Great big stars 'way up yonder,

Great big stars 'way up yonder,

Oh, my little soul's gonna shine, shine!

Oh, my little soul's gonna shine, shine!

RHYTHM PATTERNS IN A CHANT

The Circus

Marilyn Copeland Davidson

8
4
*
Let's hur - ry down to the cir - cus now!
See the el - e-phants take a bow.
Jug-gler on a tight - rope! Sil - ly, fun-ny clowns!
Bare - back rid - ers in fan - cy gowns!
Dogs do - ing danc - es! Ac - ro - bats on swings!
Oh, such fun in three mag - ic rings!

PHRASES

Find the short phrases. Find the long phrase.

MUSIC

There's music in a hammer,

There's music in a nail,

There's music in a pussy cat when you step upon her tail.

Carl Withers

Listen for short phrases. Listen for long phrases.

Old Joe

Folk Song from Texas

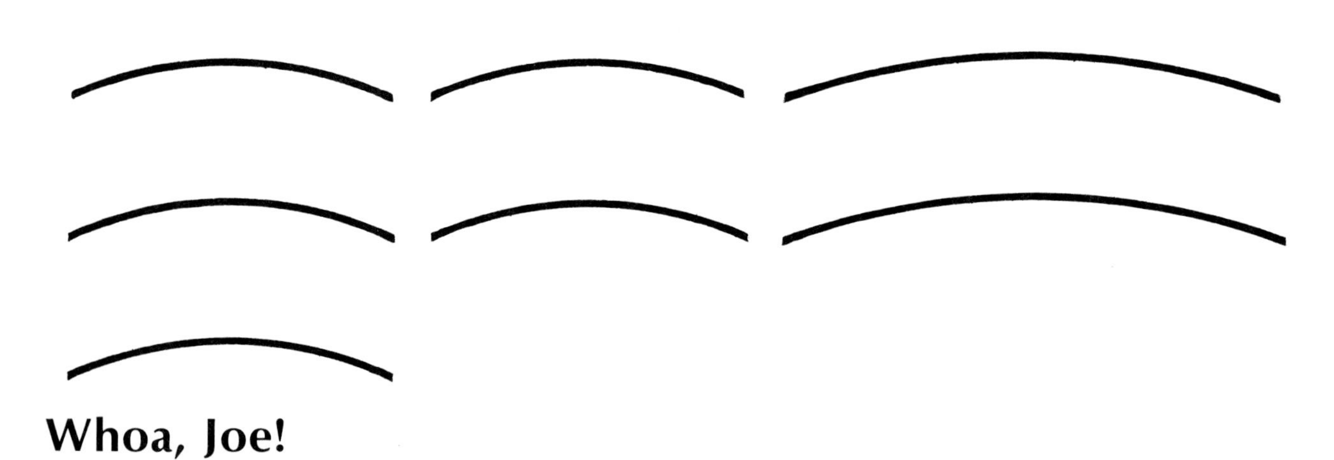

Whoa, Joe!

PHRASES IN A SONG

Follow the phrases in this music.

The Moon Is Coming Out

Children's Song from Japan English Words by Kazuo Akiyama

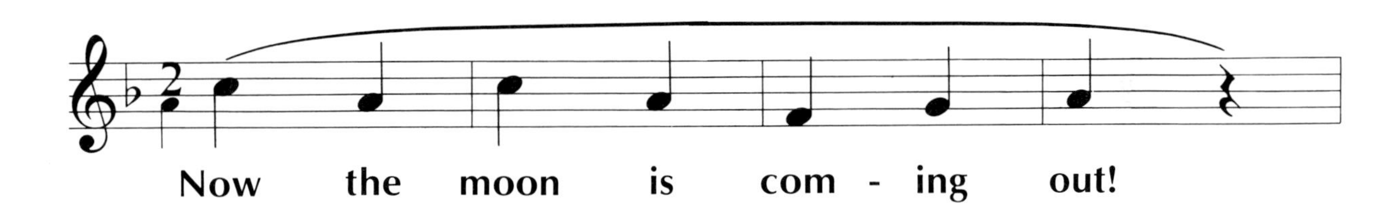
Now the moon is com - ing out!

Big and round, so big and round, as round__ as a tray.

Moon is big and round, just like a tray.

ENDINGS

Sing the ending note.

Play the ending note.

The Flea and the Mouse 8

Folk Song from Spain   English Words by Jacqueline Froom

1. There was once a flea

who loved a pretty mouse.

But they could not marry

for they had no ?

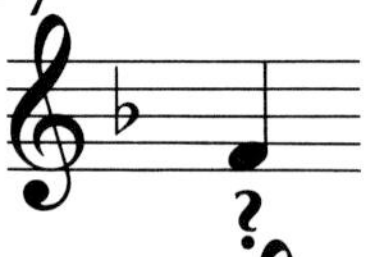

Fiddle dee, fiddle doh, fiddle ?

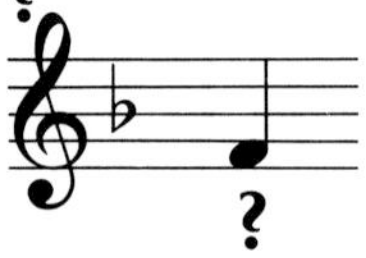

2. There was once a pig

who loved a pretty snake.

But they could not marry

for they had no ?

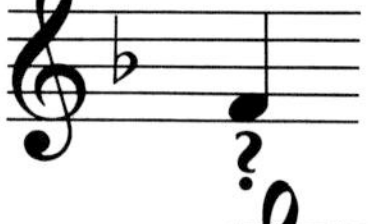

Fiddle dee, fiddle doh, fiddle ?

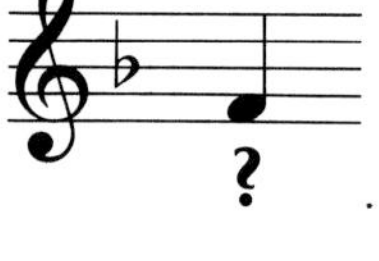

A SOUND PIECE

STREET MUSIC

Joyce Bogusky-Reimer

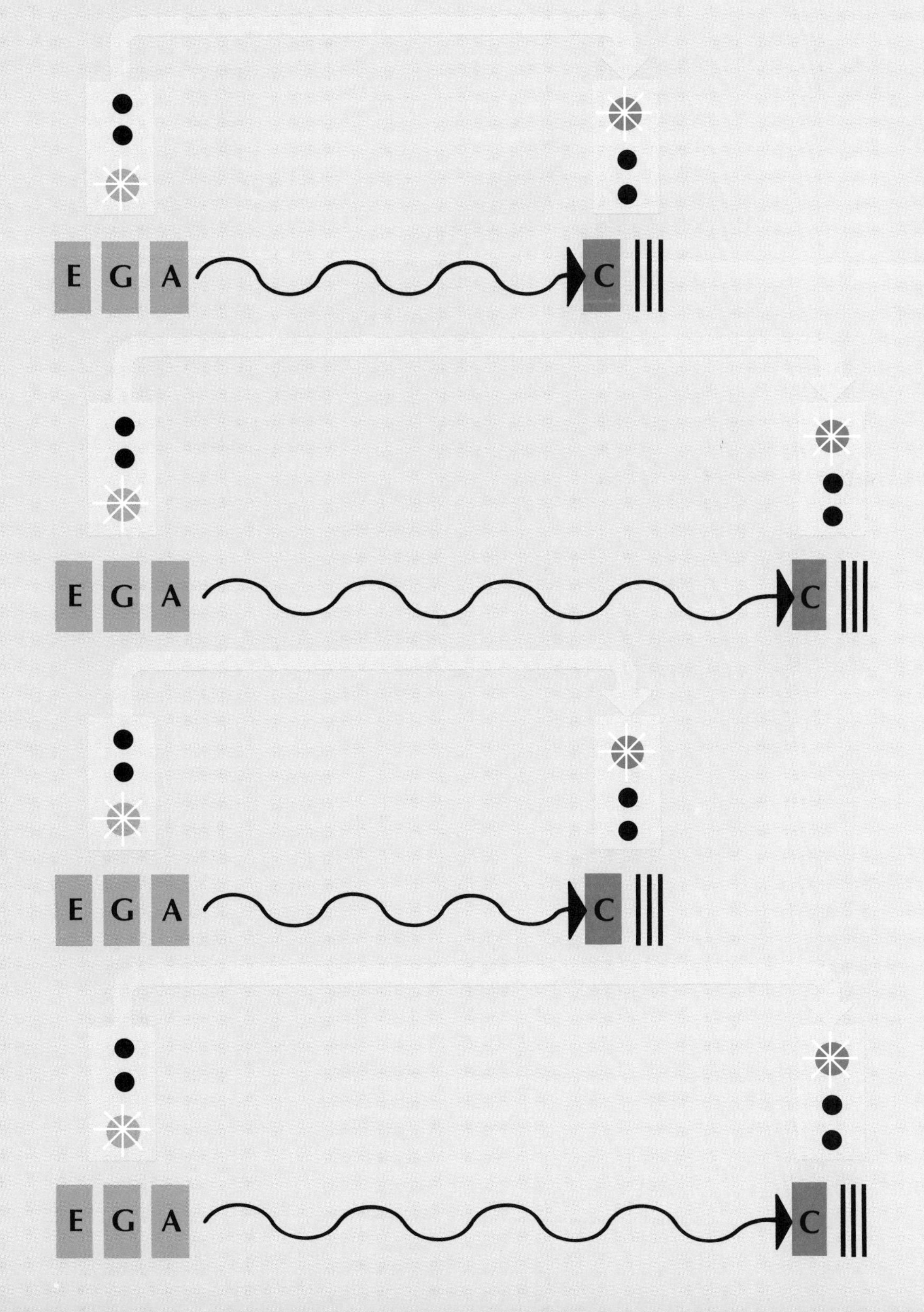
E
G
A
C
E
G
A
C
E
G
A
C
E
G
A
C

THE ARTS

1502

Which painting shows one thing?

Many things?

DETAIL OF "THE PEACEABLE KINGDOM," EDWARD HICKS. WORCESTER ART MUSEUM, WORCESTER, MASSACHUSETTS.

HARMONY

Sing a melody alone.

1.

Now add harmony.

2.

Add harmony to songs you know.

Who I Am

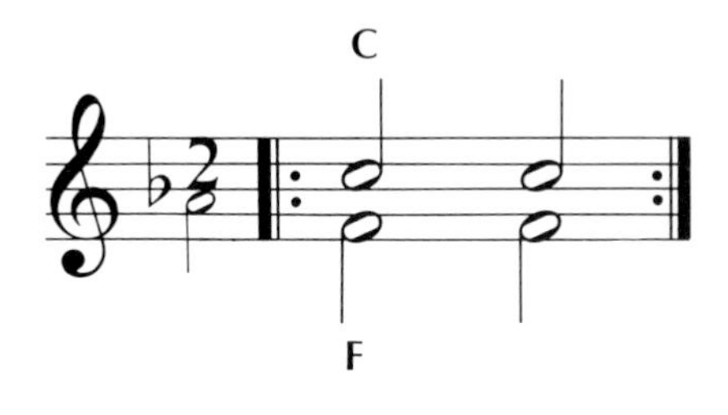
C
F

Barnacle Bill

1.

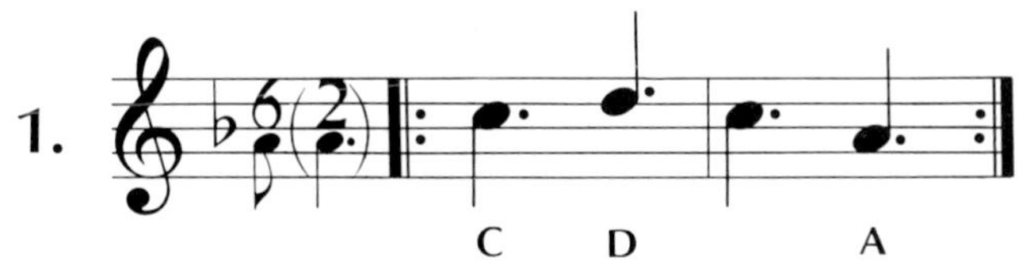
C D A

2.

F C

Clap Your Hands

1.

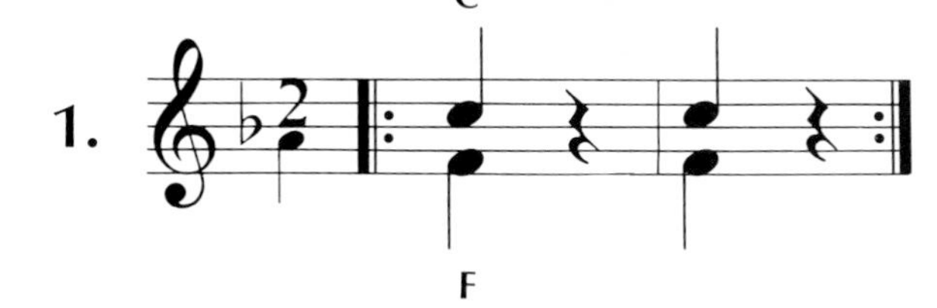
C
F

2.

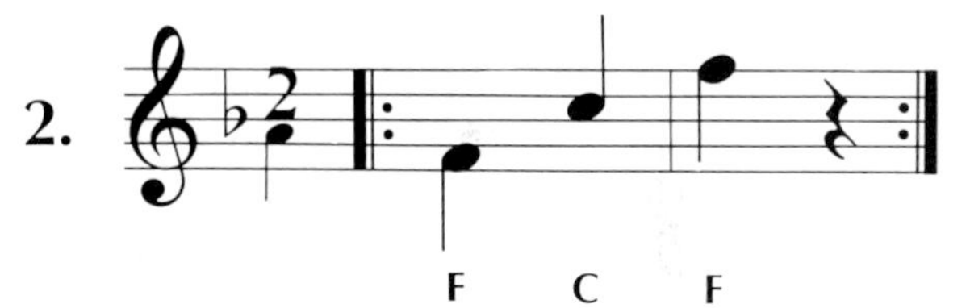
F C F

Never Sleep Late Any More

G D

I'm Gonna Sing

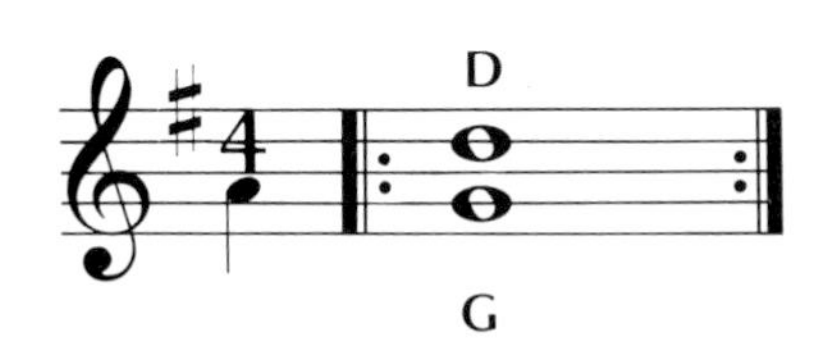
D
G

STYLE

How are the girls' clothes alike?
How are they different?
How are the boys' clothes alike?
How are they different?

HOW TONES MOVE

Which bell part shows repeated tones?

1.

G

2.

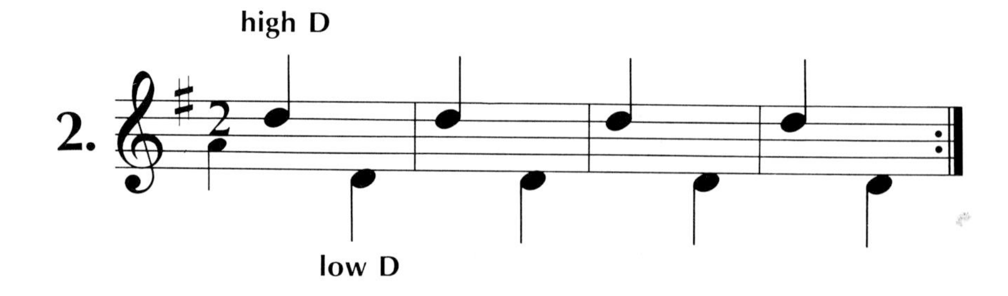
high D
low D

3.

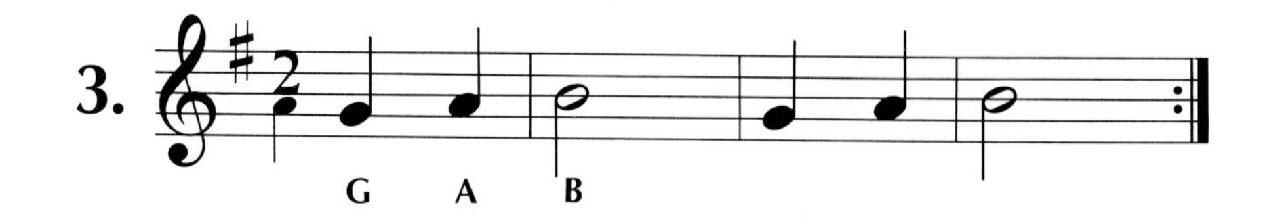
G
A
B

Which part shows tones moving by step?

Which one shows leaps from high to low?

Play one of the parts with "Ringing Bells."

Ringing Bells

Folk Song from Germany English Words by Trudi Eichenlaub

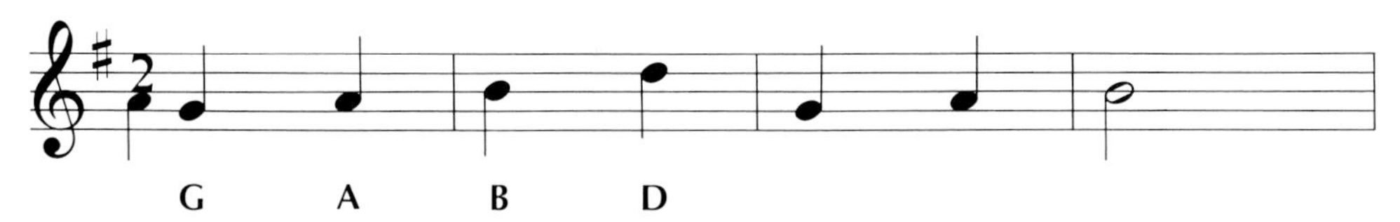
G
A
B
D

1. Sounds of bells are in the air:

2. Time to wake up, morn - ing's here:

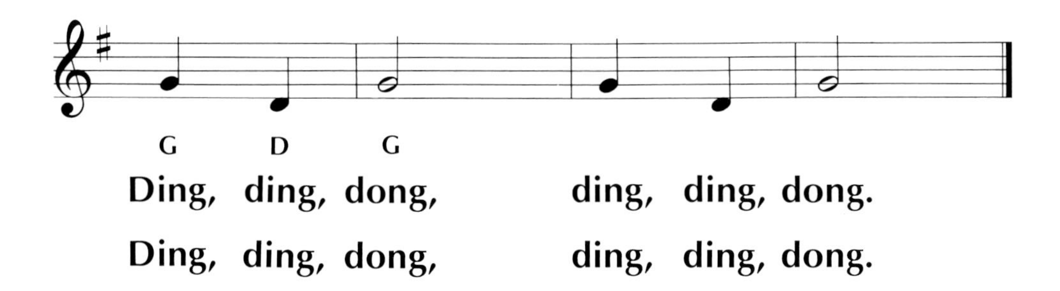
G
D
G
Ding, ding, dong, ding, ding, dong.
Ding, ding, dong, ding, ding, dong.

Use what you know. Play this song on bells.

Jeremiah, Blow the Fire

Traditional

high C
G
A
G
Je - re - mi - ah, blow the fire.

E
D
low C
Puff! Puff! Puff!

HOW MUSIC SOUNDS

What do you think will be in the mystery box?

1	2	3	4	5	6	7	?
C	D	E	F	G	A	B	?

Play this row of sounds on bells.

Does it sound finished at the end?

F B D C G A E

1.
2.

SONGS FOR YOU AND ME

Hello, Ev'rybody

Words and Music by Eunice Holsaert and Charity Bailey

Find the patterns in blue color boxes.

How many do you see?

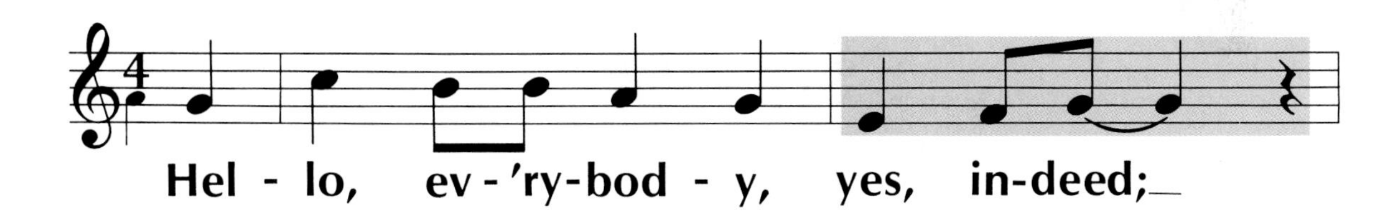
Hel - lo, ev - 'ry-bod - y, yes, in-deed;

Yes, in-deed; yes, in-deed.

Let's make mu - sic, yes, in-deed;

Yes, in-deed, my dar - ling.

Lost My Gold Ring

Children's Song from Jamaica

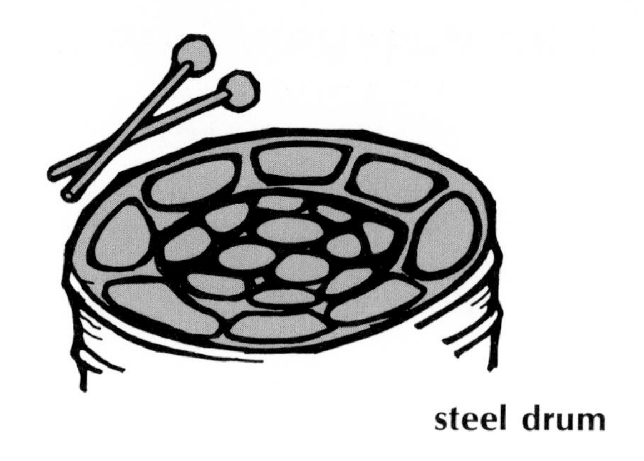
steel drum

Feel the beat as you play this singing game.

Bid - dy, Bid - dy, hold on, lost my gold ring;

One go to Kings - ton, come back a - gain.

Which instrument will you play?

G
wood block

maracas

bell

The Pawpaw Patch

Singing Game from Kentucky

Move to the beat in this singing game.

1. Where, oh where is dear lit - tle Mar - y?
Where, oh where is dear lit - tle Mar - y?
Where, oh where is dear lit - tle Mar - y?
Way down yon-der in the paw - paw patch.

2. Come on, boys, and let's go find her,

3. Pickin' up pawpaws, puttin' 'em in a basket,

Play steady beats on the bells.

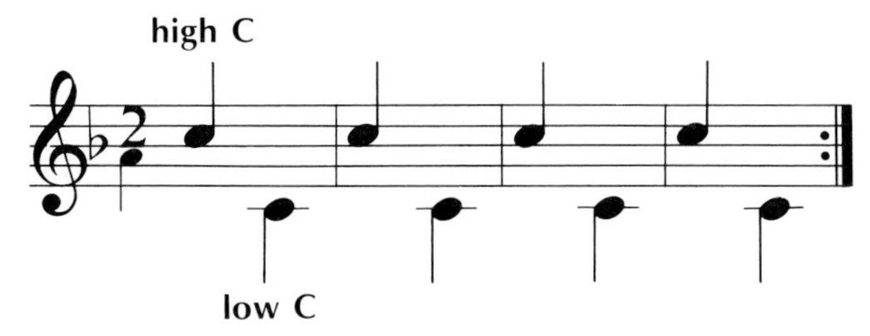
high C
low C

Piñón, pirulín

Children's Song

Who will be Miguel in this singing game?

1.,3. Pi - ñón, pi - ñón, pi - ñón,

Pi - ru - lín, pi - ru - lín, pi - ru - le - ro;

Pi - ñón, pi - ñón, pi - ñón,

Pi - ru - lín, pi - ru - lín, pi - ru - lón.

2. Miguel, Miguel, Miguel,
Turn and clap with the one on your right now;
Miguel, Miguel, Miguel,
Turn and clap with the one on your left.

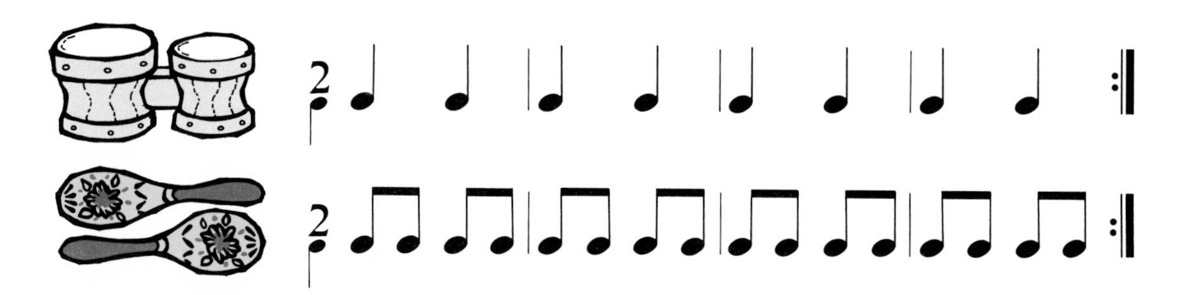

What Shall We Do?

Game Song

What will you do when you go out?

Make up your own words to sing.

1. What shall we do when we all go out,
All go out, All go out;
What shall we do when we all go out,
When we all go out to play?

2. We will climb an apple tree,

3. We will ride our bikes around,

Grinding Song

Native American Song

Which voice sings on the recording?

Hah wil lah say nehm mah say pnt, mm mm.
Say qwehn nah say nehm mah say pnt, mm mm.
Hah way way wuht nah way wuht, mm mm.
Hah way way wuht nah way wuht, mm mm.

Listen for the sticks on the recording.

Can you play the stick part?

If You're Happy

Traditional

Where are the accents in this song?

1. If you're hap-py and you know it, clap your hands (clap, clap);

If you're hap - py and you know it, clap your hands (clap, clap);

If you're hap - py and you know it,

Then your face will sure - ly show it;

If you're hap - py and you know it, clap your hands (clap, clap).

2. If you're happy and you know it, tap your foot;
3. If you're happy and you know it, nod your head;
4. If you're happy and you know it, do all three;

Going to Boston

American Play-Party Song

In which section will you strut, run, and jump?

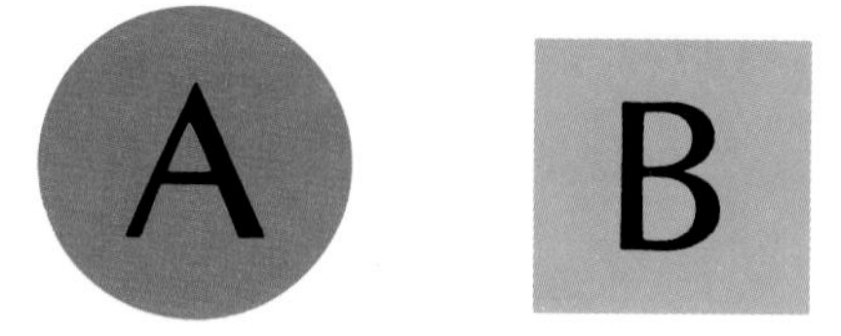
A
B

A
1.–3. Come a - long, girls, boys, we're going to Bos - ton,
Come a - long, girls, boys, we're going to Bos - ton,
Come a - long, girls, boys, we're going to Bos - ton,
Ear - ly in the morn - ing.

B

1. Don't we look jolly when we're strutting? (3 times)
   Early in the morning.
2. Don't we look jolly when we're running?
3. Don't we look jolly when we're jumping?

Hey, Betty Martin

American Folk Song

In which section will you tiptoe?

In which section will you swing?

A
B
A

A
REFRAIN
Hey, Bet-ty Mar-tin, tip-py toe, tip-py toe,
Hey, Bet-ty Mar-tin, tip-toe fine;
Hey, Bet-ty Mar-tin, tip-py toe, tip-py toe,
Hey, Bet-ty Mar-tin, please be mine.

B Swing with me, I'll swing with you,
We'll go swinging the whole day through.
Swing so fine, swing so fine,
Swinging, swinging all the time. (Refrain)

Shake My Hand

Danish Folk Song   Words Adapted by Gladys Tipton and Beatrice Landeck

Which color box shows high sounds?

Which color box shows low sounds?

1. Shake my hand and then go clap, clap, clap.

Shake my foot and then go tap, tap, tap.

One, two, three, and take a lit - tle hop,

So, we will dance un - til the mu - sic stops!

2. Shake my fingers, then go snap, snap, snap.
   Shake my knuckles, then go rap, rap, rap.
   Four, five, six, and take a little hop,
   Then whirl around until the music stops!

Noble Duke of York

Play-Party Game

Play the ending of this song on bells.

Will you play upward, or downward?

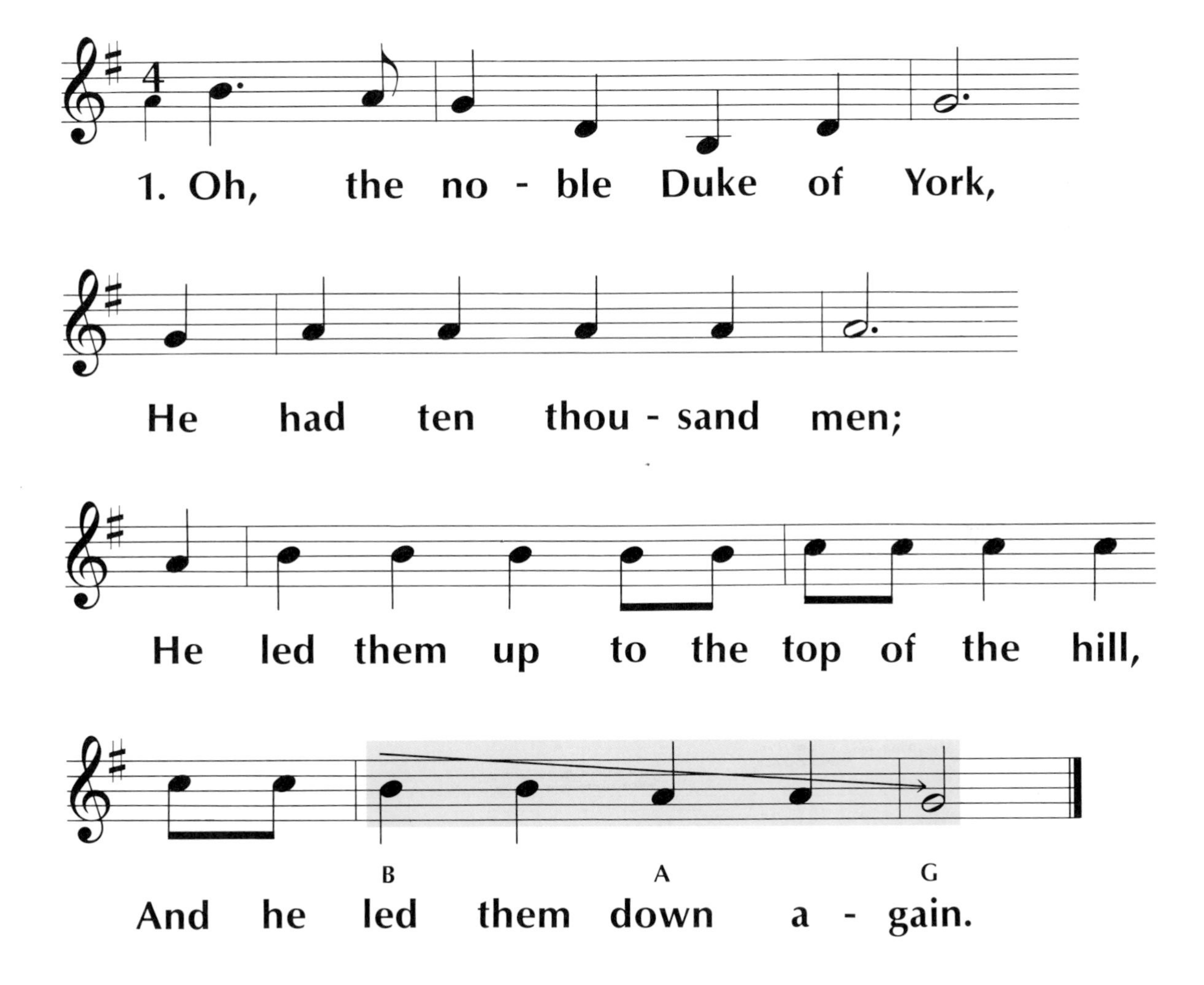
4
1. Oh, the no - ble Duke of York,
He had ten thou - sand men;
He led them up to the top of the hill,
B
A
G
And he led them down a - gain.

2. Now, when we're up, we're up;
And when we're down, we're down;
And when we're only halfway up,
We're neither up nor down.

Walk Along, John

American Folk Song

Can you play the notes in the color boxes?

Which bells will you need?

A
Come on, boys, and hush your talk - ing,

All join hands and let's go walk - ing.

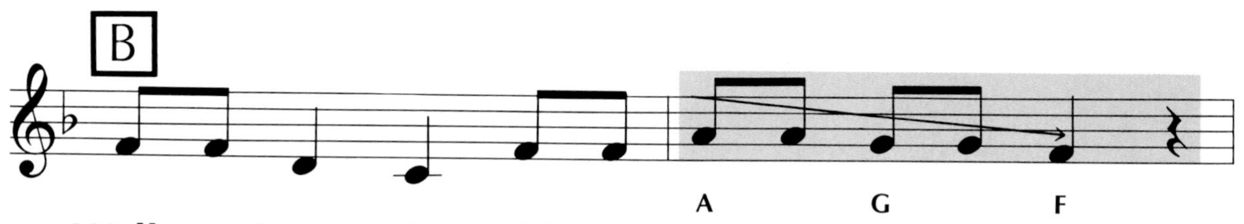
B
A G F
Walk a - long, John, with your pa - per col - lar on,

A G F
Walk a - long, John, with your pa - per col - lar on.

Up on the Housetop

Words and Music by Benjamin R. Hanby

Find the rhythm pattern in the color boxes.

Its sound is short-short-long: ♩ ♩ 𝅗𝅥

Can you hear the same pattern in section B?

A VERSE
1. Up on the house-top the rein-deer pause,
Out jumps good old San-ta Claus;
Down through the chim-ney with lots of toys,
All for the lit-tle ones' Christ-mas joys.

B REFRAIN

Ho, ho, ho, who wouldn't go!
Ho, ho, ho, who wouldn't go!
Up on the housetop, click, click, click,
Down through the chimney with good Saint Nick.

Wishy Washy Wee

American Folk Song

Find the notes in the color boxes.

Play them on bells.

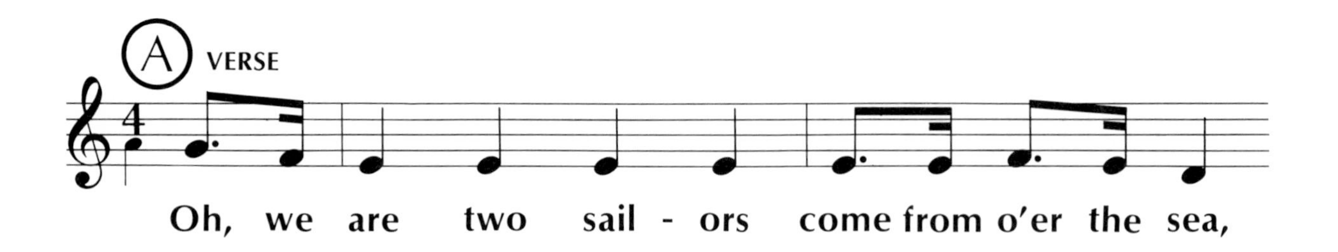

A
VERSE
Oh, we are two sail - ors come from o'er the sea,

G F E D C
If you want to go a - way a - gain, come a - long with me.

B
REFRAIN
Oh, wish - y wash - y, wish - y wash - y, wish - y wash - y wee,

G F E D C
If you want to go a - way a - gain, come a - long with me.

Up the Hickory

American Folk Song

10

Look at the notes in the color boxes.

Do they move upward, or downward?

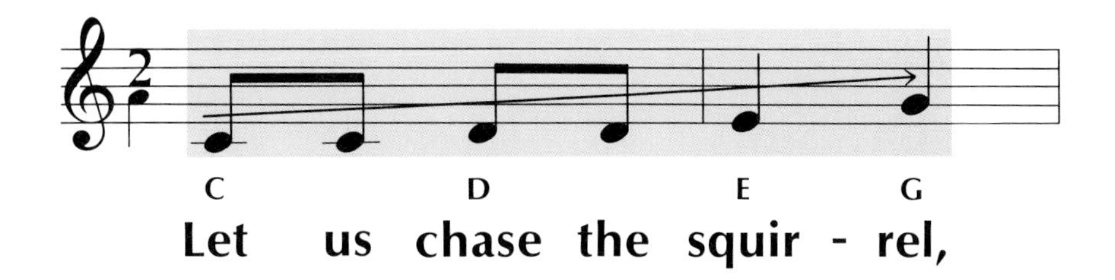
C D E G
Let us chase the squir - rel,

Up the hick - o - ry, down the hick - o - ry,

C D E G
Let us chase the squir - rel,

Up the hick - o - ry tree.

Play the upward melody on bells.

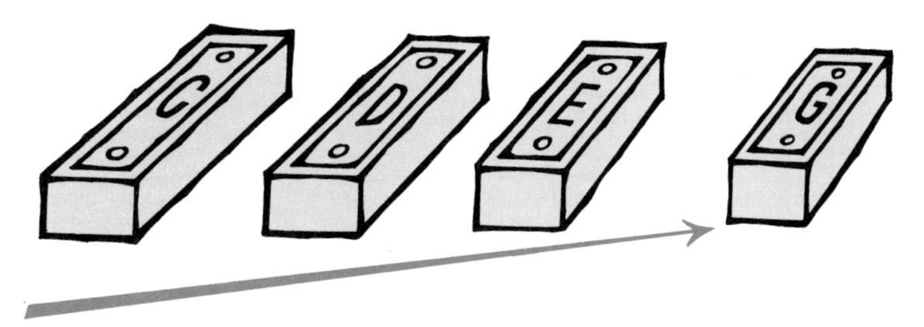
C
D
E
G

Index

Acknowledgments

Credit and appreciation are due publishers and copyright owners for use of the following.

"Music" from *A Rocket in My Pocket* compiled by Carl Withers. Copyright 1948 by Carl Withers. Reprinted by permission of Holt, Rinehart and Winston, Inc. and The Bodley Head (published in the UK by The Bodley Head).

"Thunder" by Glenys Van Every, from *Miracles,* collected by Richard Lewis. Copyright © 1966 by Richard Lewis. Reprinted by permission of Simon & Schuster, a Division of Gulf & Western Corporation.

Picture Credits

Cover: Silver Burdett
2: Victoria Beller-Smith for Silver Burdett. 3: Victoria Beller-Smith for Silver Burdett; except *b.r.,* Dan De Wilde for Silver Burdett. 4: *t.* E. R. Degginger; *m.l.* Victoria Beller-Smith for Silver Burdett; *m.r.* Al Freni; *b.* Leonard Lee Rue III/Monkmeyer Press. 5: *t.l.* T. Nebbia/DPI; *b.l.* Al Freni; *r.* Robert Perron. 6: Victoria Beller-Smith for Silver Burdett. 7: *t.l.* © Mark Boulton/National Audubon Society Collection/Photo Researchers, Inc.; *t.m.* Hille Kleinstra/Shostal Associates; *t.r.* Len Jossel; *m.* Victoria Beller-Smith for Silver Burdett; *b.l., b.m.* E. R. Degginger; *b.r.* (*t.l.*) George Roos; *b.r.* (*t.r., b.*) Angelo Focaccio. 8: *t.l., t.r.* © 1985 Wally McNamee/Woodfin Camp & Associates; *b.l., b.r.* Jerry Wachter/Focus on Sports. 10–13: Victoria Beller-Smith for Silver Burdett. 14: Victoria Beller-Smith for Silver Burdett; except *t.,* Dan De Wilde for Silver Burdett. 15–17: Victoria Beller-Smith for Silver Burdett. 18: The Pierpont Morgan Library. 19: *b.* Alfred Eisenstaedt/Life Magazine, © Time Inc. 20, 22: Victoria Beller-Smith for Silver Burdett. 24: H. A. Helmers/Shostal Associates. 25: Robert Perron. 26–27: Victoria Beller-Smith for Silver Burdett; ballerina Gwendolyn Smith, student, School of American Ballet. 30–32: Victoria Beller-Smith for Silver Burdett. 33: *t.l., m.l.* Victoria Beller-Smith for Silver Burdett; *b.l., r.* Dan De Wilde for Silver Burdett. 34–35: Victoria Beller-Smith for Silver Burdett. 36–37: Collection Walker Art Center, Minneapolis. Gift of T. B. Walker Foundation. 38, 42–43, 46: Victoria Beller-Smith for Silver Burdett. 48: Photographed by Robert E. Mates. 49: © Katherine Young. 58: "Feldhase" ("The Rabbit") by Dürer, Graphische Sammlung, Albertina, Vienna. 60: Victoria Beller-Smith for Silver Burdett. 61: *t.* Silver Burdett; *b.* Victoria Beller-Smith for Silver Burdett. 62–63: Silver Burdett Library. 63: *r.* Victoria Beller-Smith for Silver Burdett. 64: © Hamilton Wright/Photo Researchers, Inc. 66–68: Victoria Beller-Smith for Silver Burdett.

1 2 3 4 5 6 7 8 9 10—RRD—90 89 88 87 86 85 84 83